Published in Sydney

Love Notes: Poetry & Prose
I.W

ISBN   978-0-6454545-5-0

Copyright © 2023 I.W

This publication is copyright. Other than for the purposes of and subject to the conditions under the Copyright Act, no part of this publication may in any form or by any means (electronic, mechanical, micro-copying, photocopying, recording or otherwise) be reproduced, distributed, stored in a retrieval system or transmitted without prior written permission of the publisher.

Also by I.W

POETRY

Lifting the Veil (under the pseudonym I.K.Williams)

love notes

Poetry & Prose
I.W

a prelude on the second poetic concerto
(*arranged for solo poet*)

a first note

I became a musician by pure chance and a poet by pure inclination. The story of how I became a violinist began when I, aged 4 years old, started lessons at a dance school. My memory is vague in recalling some sort of plain hall with simple wooden floorboards and a teacher of some description, with a tight bun of hair spun atop her head. But I can certainly recall the reason as to why I left: as with many people at that time, the teacher and the other parents there hadn't understood how to cater for my life-threatening allergy. My mother alerted everyone about it after noticing a spread of peanut butter sandwiches on a table in the hall, politely asking if they could be removed for my safety. It was all too difficult; but eating peanut butter sandwiches and wiping their little hands everywhere, my fellow dancers weren't safe to be around.

So I had to change careers.

My mother noted that no musician ever seemed to eat around their instrument and so, being deemed safe, I picked up my first violin at age 5.

I'm not sure when I picked up my first pen but I remember writing my first poems in school and absolutely falling in love with forming words. I worked for years on sentences and stanzas before finally producing my first collection of poems, 'Lifting the Veil'.

And so, I have always had a special love for notes and nouns. As a musician and a poet, I wanted to meld the two into a collection about romance, rhythm and relationships. This is the book you now hold in your hands. Flick through it, glancing any poem that comes to you, or read it cover to cover.

Regardless, I hope it imparts that feeling of love we all deeply desire and sparks the memory of something special in your heart.

with love,
I.W

bars

the first movement—da capo

faith

where I first learnt what love is

drifting

what mothers do

zeroes + ones

falling apples

self-portrait

tangled earphones

simple time

the cake

on her own

the second movement—andante con molto

picking petals

wishing for you

first meeting

connection

thoughts over coffee

love notes

the third movement—allegro con brio

love me at allegro

daydreams

the reasons why

something tender about the breeze

scary

eyes on the road

stories

the fourth movement—dolente

lost me

change

busker

a trip into town during the pandemic

withdrawals

missing

siren

shattered glass

katie

cavity

blue

final

ghost town

colours (let me go)

out of print

clover

a night in November (empty shells)

lost property

a portrait of you

encore—con amore

the words

I promise

~~little~~ big girl

the first movement

da capo

"from the beginning"

faith

You
były
baptised
in the Autumn
-when the leaves fell
and changed their colours-
but you stood tall as a tree;
your
roots
planted
deep.

where I first learnt what love is

It was here — under the flight path, under ever-sunned days that I first learnt what love is.

It's a 'thank you' to the fake food service from the wood cubby house. It's the patience with that croaking violin, emanating from the back room. It's watching us run bare of clothes through a sprinkler and smiling at us as we wave. It's the handcrafted dolls house filled with teeny furniture that took him months to make.

It was here, yes here, that I remember it. That first concert with that tiny instrument in my tiny hands. 'Twinkle Twinkle Little Star'. The uplifted bow, held high above for my signature finish.

And it was here: that first friend at that first school in the first grade. When she moved away, love was there to console my crying.

Love was their belief – that first ride through the park on the red-pink path without the training wheels.

It was here, it was here, on the corner.
The brick and the pickets.
The front door in the wrong street
(according to our address.)
The little dog with her head through the gate.
The wagging tail.
The wail of a twin tantrum.

Love was home, and home was family.
It was here, where I first learnt what love is.

drifting

I'm unsure how this came to be—
this gift of grand green-blue,
stretching to the horizon's line.
And how grateful I should be to travel these seas—
sailor like everyone else, yet somehow, I don't yet
appreciate their majesty, their movement and motion.

I'm unsure how this came to be—
years later, this feeling.
I feel, for a while now, I've been

        d r i   f   t   i   n   g

                                      as

                                driftwood,

        washing in and out with a winded tide.
    Life, all my days, tinge of turbulence, my focal eye
              on the brewing storms overhead and
                    not a calming, collecting current.

And I'm unsure, oh unsure how this came to be—
this fear of deep water, this stressing over storms,
this hatred of salt, simply for fear of stinging sensations
that are meant to do me good: heal me, not harm.

But

her arms.

I remember how her arms would once surround me.
Never unsure.

A mother 'ship'— cradling, carrying, lulling me to sleep.
A hull holding firm against the thrashing, the crash of
angry waves outside.

And her song: alluring as a siren,
but instead of a *doomed* drowning,
I would drown in the devoted depths of her love.

I must remember that.
That and her ardent advice:
that these oceans, these bowels of brine;
though chasmic, chaotic, crashing against my mind—
are something I can weather.

For now though, for now,
I drift along as a wind-struck feather.
Not knowing the shore on which I shall arrive.

I am still

           d
        r
      i

            f
                t
              i
                    n
                          g

                                    as driftwood.

what mothers do

When my mind raced and I fell apart,
and I felt ocean blue,
I said: "Why don't you love me?"
You said: "Sweetheart, you know I do."
And I know that's true—
for that moment you breathed me out
and I began to coo,
I gurgled without comprehension
but your heart was all I knew.

And each of our first words
and steps and birthdays,
you'd celebrate like a debut.
I didn't recognise it then
but you really cared for us two.

Growing up grew tougher
but never did your love and care.
I don't think I acknowledged it then,
but you were always reasonable and fair.

When I returned home too late
or stayed up on my phone,
I know I've never said this,
but I'm thankful for your tone.

And when I left home,
I know wholly, your love is true,
because I said:
"Don't worry about me."
And you said:
"But that's what mothers do."

zeroes + ones

```
/* He once told me of zeroes and ones.
(As it turns out, he doesn't just speak
in notes.)

It was clear as reflection that he had
surpassed me; like how the horizon
surpasses those boats.

You see, now he's no longer drifting.
Instead, he's sifting the flour and
coding away the hours. Offering mum hand-
plucked flowers.

I try to decode it sometimes;
this language of numbers he knows,
but it's so clear that I'm inadequate
here-- so clear 'cos I only know verse.

There were times when I saw only the
worst in the twin I argued with, but we
have grown so much-- from 0 to 1 before
our eyes.

And his eyes: hazy green
are enveloped by the screen.
Does he dream in the realm of machine?
It hardly matters: (he's having fun).

Having fun with zeroes and ones. Horizons
surpassing and goal-setting suns. My boat
has tipped but to my rescue he comes; the
brother who speaks in zeroes and ones.
  */
```

falling apples

She's in a type of trance,
in Dungiven, sitting with schoolbags as crooked
climbers pinch from the overarching branch.
Their loot is forbidden fruit
despite the absence of snakes to goad them on.

The apple-neglecting,
all-round-respecting,
school-bag-inspecting 'saint' walks by,
and my, oh my, oh my—
the knowledge they'll one day die
is keen in his saintly eye.

They're sent to his office for the cane.
Slaps of the hand like hammered nails.
Wails protrude from the sinners mouths
yet she is quiet for he allowed
her simply chastisement for minding the bags.

Our patience lags
as she recites again
her story of apple theft
yet we still pretend it's our first occasion hearing it.

"I love you Grandma"
Her look – confused.
"It was lovely to meet you" she says.
And with that, we know someone's been picking—
picking off her memories: red and ripe.
Her tree of connections is yielding less fruit.
She's forgetting the wrong and the right.

But the light is still there
in her Irish eyes,
though age is hard to bare,
we know its price—
she will forget us and apples too
but we'll tend to her garden,
even as she utters, "Who?"

I hope we don't fall far from her—
this Eve of our family.
I'll always remember her story
of minding bags by an apple tree.

self-portrait

Mustard jumper (oversized.)
Sleeps with a stuffed toy (not her man.)
Always spouting stupid jokes.
Cooking usually from a labelled can.

Plays Bach (poor intonations.)
Writes poems no-one reads.
Overdoes her explanations.
Feels sick over immoral deeds.

Always a pen in her handbag.
Always a word on her tongue.
Haircut: fringe and brown.
Sings in the shower about 'the one'.

Works part-time and dreams the rest.
Blue-grey eyes fixate on her phone.
Her mouth almost always moving.
Greatest fear: being alone.

tangled earphones

Looking back I realise:
you were music to my blocked ears.
Sweet symphonic sound,
a fermata s tre t c h i n g years...

And looking back now I realise:
these moments were at the time, to me, a noisy drone.
These memories I'd so quickly disregard,
as one does their tangled earphones.

But in reality this clamorous piece,
this tangled mess of memory,
is all I want to repeat,
is all I want to repeat :|

Because the beat of this world is out of tempo,
and its Conductor has fallen asleep.
They so quickly disregard love and faith and hope,
and then stupidly wonder why they weep.

Keep.
How I want to keep that lullaby
with which dad would sing me to sleep,
and that silly song we made when we were seven:
the hallowed sounds of a far off Heaven.

Looking back now, oh looking back,
though those moments were to me
once a noisy drone.
I will tackle the tangled memories,
restore them—
just like those tangled earphones.

simple time

Conductor,
if I'm being honest, it's been years.
Years since I've known myself
and where I come from.

Take me back there—
to the simple time.
Where everything was four bars and four beats.
Where each street
spoke a memory to my listening ear.
'Cos Conductor, now I cannot hear.
I cannot read their music anymore.

It's not dead —no, it's not— but
these places, these pieces feel less alive now.
As though their fingers have fallen asleep,
gone all fuzzed
and now this childhood orchestra
is pins and needles.

Dear Conductor, where's your baton?
Where's your guiding gesture?
Your 1 and 2 and 3 and 4 and…?
Where have the beats gone? Where's time fled to?

'Cos Conductor
I can't play as well anymore.
That violin sits in the studio,
barely breathing in its coffin case.

Take me back there— to the place
where we would sing from stages,
rummage through score pages,
our ages: not touching the double digits.

Take me back there.
Take me back.
Take me
to the simple time.

the cake

|| | ||| |||
|| || ||

These years, they lie
on a plastic plate — coated in sugar,
made for gaining weight. And I barely taste
it now, this confectionary cake, but as slices turn to
crumbs, I'll realise my mistake. For these are the sweet
days, the birthdays of my youth —and while I've always
held a more savoury tooth—I'll find myself wishing for
more filling and more cream, as each candle

---

melts away just as childhood dreams.

on her own

It's funny how words change us—
she tries them on like clothes.
Today she feels like a summery dress
instead of the winter woollen her mother chose.

Lately, she's been trying on vocabulary,
changing in and out of phrases.
From 'on her own' to 'in her own';
each new 'fit like a thesaurus' pages.

In stages, in stages she rehearses the syllables.
Each vowel.
Each con-son-ant.
A rant
about being single,

by herself

but then a chant
about being free.

She is free and in her own,
though she is alone.
That loneliness that sets in,
in which she's stuck; like a grandfather
to a leather armchair.

She's unknowing, so unaware
of how these things will all soon change.
She's a novelist with a fresh book:
written with old words, but in an order that's newly
arranged.

She is 'on her own' but '*in* her own'—
almost antonyms, opposite phrases.
She goes through stages,
sitting at the back of her quiet library mind,
searching for meaning
in dictionary pages.

If only she knew,
if only she
could turn to her book's last sentence.
Then she'd see
that it's okay to be lonely.
It's okay to be

                                        on her own

the second movement

andante con molto

"slowly with motion"

picking petals

It seems to you love is a matter of 'yes' or 'no'.
"Does he love me, or is it not so?"
You plucked off the petals, seeking to know.
but just like flowers, love, it grows.

And sometimes, love, over time, it slows—
a flower, wilting, down toward ground it goes.
But your soul knows, your soul, soul knows
if they will fill you or just add to your woes.

Don't pick petals—
'cos they're from Chance's garden.
Only your inner self sees
if your heart will harden.
Just let the seeds planted bear
the fruit they are granted.

Because love is a matter of 'let it grow'.
Let it grow or let it be so.

wishing for you

For the man
who will, with loving eyes, look.
Who will laugh when he learns I can hardly cook.
For him, who will my open hand, hold.
Who will beside me, stand,
even as I grow gracelessly old.

For the man
who, in tender moments,
will make time itself pause.
Who will watch our children's concerts and grant
them vigorous applause.

Who will just as I am, cherish me
(even when I speak my mind.)
Who will ages onward, only goodness see
(even when he's going blind.)

For the man
who will under his breath,
softly mutter lullabies and our song.
Who will cause my heart to flutter,
even as decades drift along.
For the man
who will love my soul
as the counterpoint to his own.
Who will tend weekly with refreshed flowers,
to my tired, lonesome headstone.

For the man
who will so lovingly speak
of memories aged and greying.
Who will comfort, console our family
when he sees troubles, are weighing.

For him, who will move onward:
driven, bright and strong.
Who will teach our dear grandchildren,
the discernment
of right and wrong.

For the man, for the man,
for whom I tenderly wish.
Take my hand, take my heart
with one romantic swish.
Please, love me tender in all your ways.
Be mine, I'll be yours for all our days.

first meeting

For what felt like centuries, Loneliness was my only friend. But she sat
In her solace and pretended I wasn't there. After a while,
Reality sunk his fanged teeth deep into my chest and I
Struggled to comprehend
Truth. But then, unexpectedly, I

Met you.
Eras of emptiness
Evaporated like warmed water left in the desert day. Somehow
That initial connection of irises, that singular searching of souls in that one moment,
Ignited a flame of faith in me; faith that I could fall, fall into someone with
No fear of pavements or ground. And resound, does the pounding muscle in my chest— with a vitality I've yet to know. I know, I've only just met you, but I cannot wait to see how this
Goes...

connection

First
there's that eye lock— two circles embracing the eerie blackness and the rim of greeny blue around them.

Then, the words —roaming in spacious thought— are plucked into being, into syllables: audible on the tongue. A gentle laugh welcomes way for hearty chuckles, vibrations and quivering earth. The fingers graze each other: a brief second of seismic activity.

thoughts over coffee

You and coffee have a lot in common—
a grim taste with a scent
that's deceivingly, deceptively nice.
You're both hard to get used to
yet addictive once you do,
and you go well with something sweet;
like myself or a slice.

You both keep me awake till late hours,
and you scold me if I hold you too long.

You and coffee,
you and coffee,
you and coffee.

You both taste oh so strong.

love notes

I was *fine.* before you.
Playing in my own key——
wasn't seeking song,
wasn't hearing symphony.

But then I heard your single note,

a chord struck,
a composition you wrote
for my heart—-
not a solo part
but a harmony line
to your melody.

And we danced to your song
for hours long—-
the beat: our out of tempo hearts.
Before you was an anacrusis,
before you: just a prelude start.

Never did I know
music's swift dynamic shifts.
From your whispered *pianissimo* to
your *forte* touch upon my lips.

And in the grips of rhythm,
our love notes dotted 'cross the page,
I feel so soprano, so sharp, so high,
as our music echoes on this concert stage.

the third movement
allegro con brio
"at a fast tempo with spirit"

love me at allegro

You loved me at *allegro*—
fast-paced and *forte* and flourishing.
And you skipped all manner of rests and rhythm,
so I put our love

on pause

Silence spanning several bars.
But my bow drifted back to the strings.

A slow crescendo, a gradual *gliss.*
to the note where
we'd left off.

Some passages were tough and troubled—
they needed practice and patience and practice.
I scribbled all over our manuscript
but eventually our melody sung.

You're a great sight reader—
a natural at this.
We are sweet, soprano, sharp.
No flats in our key— only accidentals.
Can't wait to play the next bar...

daydreams

I used to weed out the wandering—
a mind that whittled away hours,
dreaming of faces that I couldn't kiss,
pining for bouquets of wedding flowers.

But now I succumb to sun-dreams,
my heart: flourishing and whole.
Because I finally met the man for me,
the one who soothes my soul.

the reasons why

It's your bright blue orbs connecting with my soul.
A sense of what seemed broken, within me,
swiftly whole.
It's your infectious laugh when we have 'too much fun'
and the deepest feeling that you are truly,
my only, only one.

It's your comfortable embrace, your gentle hand-hold.
The utterance of your lips, saying:
"I want to with you, grow old."
It's our slow dance on the beach
and our long, loving walks.
Our difficult, yet somehow easy, deep, devoted talks.

Your sharing (or rather stealing) food from my plate.
Your kindness shining through,
even from our very first date.
It's the way you hold my hair back when I am feeling ill.
The way you say I love you and how
you make time itself fall still.

It's your thoughtful gifts and yellow flowers,
how you give me your time
(though I can't quite count the hours.)
It's your gentlemanly way,
all the little things you say.

It's the meals and grace we share.
I just know how much you care!
Your prayerfulness and love of our Lord.
The way you worship with me
and how you make me feel adored.

The way we shut the world out when
we are just together.
The way you bring the best in me,
it's the feeling of forever.
And it's the butterflies in my stomach,
the way my heart just knows,
that your love is one that will not weaken
but with memories and moments grow.

All these many reasons and so many more
are why I'm so certain and sure
that our love will endure,
our hearts always pure.

Thank you, my dear shepherd,
for loving and seeing me.
I'm so thankful for you and so happy we can be.

something tender about the breeze

There's something tender about the breeze.
With ease, its gentle arms wrap about my waist.
In haste; so many run from the cool grasp
upon the skin.
The breaking out of gooseflesh scares them
as does their deadly sins.

But there's something there about the breeze
with loving fidelity, it's sure and strong.
Prolong do I my walks in the eve,
for the soft breeze provides sweet song.

No melody quite as gentle,
though sometimes quite so loud.
The breeze's piece consumes me
just as the sun envelops the cloud.

There's something there, oh something about the crisp
cool air of early dawn, the sway of stretching branches,
the day's tender yawn.

Maybe the breeze is like my love.
Always there, caressing and cradling me.
Maybe his arms reach all about
to shade me as the trees.

And maybe, the grass is as his eyes,
sharp and expansive and green.
Perhaps his smile is as the dew
with its bright and youthful gleam.

Yes he is as the breeze,
surrounding powerfully
and overwhelmingly.
Sometimes distant
as a setting sun
but always rising
to brighten me.

And frighten, oh how it frightens me:
that we might drift as leaves to the wind.
Sent upon separate waves of air.
Like the sun's glare, I detest this thought.

And heavily sought are our long walks in the eve,
for there's something tender about his breezy way.
With loving fidelity, he's sure and strong.
Prolong do I my talks with him all day.

scary

You're like Halloween night– I am frightened to close my eyes for fear of nightmares: dark visions of you. And yet, like a horror film, I watch you with my hand over my eyes, peeking and sneaking glimpses.

It's scary how I could lose you. Like a flash of electricity, Frankenstein's storm. It's unnatural how much I love you, as though I'm in a trance, or have been bitten– I'm cursed to care.

I invited you in, now I've welcomed the unknown dark.

eyes on the road

I've always been taught to have my eyes on the road: to drive safe, to avoid potholes. But you came along, stood in the middle of the highway. Now, I've got one hand on the wheel, the other on yours.

stories

With you, reality blurs with fiction
and I'm unsure if I'm writing
biographically or pretending.
I hope this isn't a novel of limited pages,
cos I know that stories
have starts but also endings.

I want to avoid planning and plotting our love,
I'll pen us with the ink-blood of my veins.
I'm not one to sit and think on chapters,
I let fluid imagination take the reins.

And stains
of ink
speckle my hand
as it holds tight to yours.
I hope we don't become just words,
just words
told as unoriginal lore…

the fourth movement
dolente

"very sorrowful"

lost me

Ever since I found you,
it's like I lost 'me'.
As though I don't know the back of my own hand
without yours upon it, don't know my own face without
the smile you've pressed into my cheeks.
And though it's only been a matter of weeks,
identity
suddenly
isn't about looking in a mirror at my reflection
nor is it introspection.

It is instead hanging onto whether or not the message
I sent you is left on read.
Living for the utterance of love
from your lips.
It's seeking the tender touch of your gentle fingertips.
Skipping, tripping over every beat of my heart
when you're away or we're apart.

I didn't realise until
someone pointed it out to me:
to be utterly, universally consumed
is to be doomed;
entombed am I by love.

change

My only true constant is change.

Today, I change
out of the black, bitter nightdress
and into Day's blouse:
white, fluffed up sleeves,
like the purest cloud.
But I do not forget the night—
for the night, I regret and I rue.
(It was eve-fall after all when I fatefully met you.)

Debt.
I'm in debt.
Horrendous debt to you.
(Maybe I can pay for it with my spare change.)
Change is strange
as these coins that I pull from the purse.
You only get change when you give too much.

Some change is so rounded, shiny and blemishless.
Others: dated, disfigured and worthless.

You know, I banked on us being the former coin.
I gave too much.
I changed for you.

busker

Begging like a busker for attention.
Like an instrument— pick me up
                         and put me down again.

I'm seeking some musical direction
'cos it seems like we've reached ***riten.***

a trip into town during the pandemic

March

This is the world
of no 'bless you' to a sneeze.
It is the silent carriage from one place to the next.
A singular cough calls through the compartment,
met with glares and stares, and

April

nobody smiles,
nobody cares.

May

Masks up.
Eyes down.

June

A woman props the bag on the seat
so you cannot sit
and she cannot hear you: (her earbuds are in.)
Dowse your hands in sanitiser
and feel those cuts sting.
No one ever said pandemics were pretty things.

July

The restrictions tighten tomorrow, midnight.
It means you cannot catch that overseas flight
and the churches cannot be bright with God's light.
Their doors are closed and their curtains drawn.
Their bells are broken, the veil is torn,
and scorn is felt by all your hearts.
You'd better get going before your bus departs.

August

A sneeze on the sidewalk as you wait.
It comes but they won't let you on.
Full capacity has been reached,
though half the seats
are empty.
And then the bus is gone.

A solitary walk to work
and every soul is distant.
You think to yourself if you
could capture old instants
where everything was normal and
everyone was close,
maybe then the world would feel better,
even without a vaccine dose.

withdrawals

Shivery. Shaky sadness.
My hand — it quivers like the branch
tapping persistent at the glass, this eerie night.
I also tap persistent at glass:
a small square of it, its glare
stunning me out of sleep.
I want to keep you
an inch from my face as I wander in
and out of Consciousness' care.

        I'm barely aware.

Barely here.
                                        Barely there.

I think I'm going through withdrawals.

missing

I lost a friend last week (but maybe it was months ago.)

For a while or so
she's been plastered across my mind
like a missing person poster:
every tree,
every street block
and everywhere I've thought to go and find,
covered by her face and thick tape.

Her portrait is black and white.

It seems to be draping;
that final curtain over our friendly days.
See, cut down is that tree we used to swing from.
Closing down is that mall where we used to shop.
The Wi-Fi signal has dropped;
the connection's lost
and our friendship: tossed
into a wastepaper basket.

And in my heart, my soul,
something not so small
is missing:
that takes a lot to admit.
To admit, it was my fault.
Maybe I held the saw against that tree.
Reality:
maybe it was me
who sent the shop into recession.
The obsession,
my heart's confession
meant I placed less priority on someone who I always
pictured was a given and granted to be close to me.

siren

You pulled me in like the tide.
Shallow waves– the cold type you
slowly shiver into.
And I waded by those waters,
but soon I was swimming,
then treading, dreading the deep.

I've never been much of a swimmer,
but those waves, your waves crashing against me,
shimmered so shiny in sunlit summer.
As a Siren, they drew me to a doomed drowning.

And I drowned deep in you,
sea salt stinging my wounds,
your water filling my lungs.

Shivering and scared,
they pulled me from your ocean.

Never again will I wade.

shattered glass

It's not right.
It's like we did it all in backward time:
exchanging details first,
then colliding, crashing apart.
He left me in shattered shambles,
strewn haphazard across the path.
Then, he left the scene.
He left.
He left me broken-boned, bereft.

Now I can't seem to find
all the pieces left behind.
My mind: a blacktop littered
with the remnants of a collision.
I was going at full speed;
didn't see his red light.
But regardless,
he should've stopped after to see,
to see I was alright.

That night
and in that moment,
time put the brakes on, hard.
And now I'm as shattered glass:
my vehicle of love permanently scarred.

katie

Katie,
I know that lately, you've been feeling as rough tides and stormy seasons. They say men come and go, that friendships shouldn't, though, ours did.

Ours did

d   r   i   f   t
        a   p   a   r   t

several months at sea, no communication between you and me, I felt lost, lonely sailor. *What did I do?*

And Katie,
it's like ocean blue, that eerie feeling of something lurking then a message bottle from you, an ancient scroll. Too late and aeons of absence took their toll.

I'm sorry I couldn't rescue you. Stranded on Isle Abandonment, on a shore of ignore-ance.

And Katie,
    Katie
    Katie
maybe I bottled it up too. Maybe I knew, maybe I knew: our friendship sought the rocks.

As clocks tick and Life's waves crash, I pray you know how much it meant. And as days disappear alongside years, our paths turning from straight to bent, I need you to know those hours spent rambling about work and clothes and boys were some of the simplest joys, the simplest joys of my seasick heart.

Katie.   K a t i e   K   a   t   i   e.

I   '   m
            s   orry

    w e
            d r i f t   e d

                    a   p   a   r   t

cavity

I don't know if I'm doing this right.
But I guess I am, because
it hurts,
it deserts,
it converts
faith to fear,
love to war.

I don't want war with you—
not after all we've been through.
The fights,
sad nights,
the bites
in our chocolate hearts.

Mine melted once for you
but now it's hardened, encased round a sour fruit.
To think our love produced such bitter tastes
but it's true—
you're better without me
and I without you.

I'm leaving,
we're grieving,
you're receiving
my truth:
you left cavities in my soul
like how candy impacts my tooth.

blue

You were the first
to touch my spirit—
you and your bright blue, vibrant eye-lights.
You roared me to life as an engine
that'd never been turned on.
It wasn't long
till we had 'our song'—
like your irises, it was electric.
Blue. Full of feeling.

Now,
my stomach's reeling at the sound of it.
It reminds me too much of you
And blue and blue. Blue…

I blew my nostrils apart over you
and the tissue box spewed
fluffed, fragmented white shrapnel.
Maybe it was stuffing—
like that you find (the innards)
when tearing up a childhood toy.
For my childhood was gone in that moment.
I'd been yet to know the ache of that
beating,
pounding,
resounding muscle implanted in my centre.

But now I knew—
my heart collapsed at the contemplation of you.

Now I'm blue:
so blue.
Oh blue.

final

I studied for you like the big final— the massive test worth half my grade. (And I thought I earnt a HD, an A+.) Despite this, the results came back marked with the big red 'F'.

I tried to repeat the exam for a better score but the teacher refused my resit request. She said,

"A test is a test, and you failed it but you tried your best."

ghost town

No one comes here anymore.
Those romantic thoughts are tumbleweeds,
dried and deserted,
swaying swift in the breeze
of this troubled town.

The heart's now a spectral spirit,

                d r i f t i n   g,

        drooping under a white sheet.

Rip off the sheet and there's nothing,
no-one there but a ghostly, vague impression.

This is the town where love once was,
now haunted only by nostalgia.

colours (let me go)

If you love me, let me go.
You know that I'm not for you.
If we were truly meant to be,
everything would be bright yellow, sky blue.

But all I see is black—
dark, inky icky night.
A cloud has cast over me,
our weather postpones plane flights.

A sickly, curdling colour,
I've been feeling greeny-brown of late.
The dramatic design of this dangerous game
keeps me up as I contemplate.

And how you must be feeling purple—
a kingly power about your speech.
You know you're anything but regal.
Though I was your subject,
you've no right to preach.

Colour leeches
from my face.
As I realise your embrace will never seize.
You'll squeeze the colours from me
till I am grey and white: deceased.

My final plea
is let me be
and please don't be red with rage.
If you love me, let me go.
You're not colourblind,
this black and white image
you can gauge.

out of print

My love, we went out of print years ago—
there's no room for us on the shelf anymore.
Though, I did find an old copy in this second hand
store, our spine bent and battered and beaten.

My love, we were a page-turner,
a cliff-hanger read.
And oh, hasn't enough been said?
Why does love beg to be a bestseller book
when most novels aren't even half-read?

clover

No more.
It is over.
I picked you like a four-leafed clover
but just my luck: it wasn't meant to be.

The clover never actually had four leaves, but three.

a night in November (empty shells)

I watch the twilight trickle in through the slither of
glass, wrapped in curtain.
This was the time, our time —
we used to catch the sunset on a walk round
our tiny town.
But now
I crouch

alone

over a notebook, in a dimly lit dark, a night in
November that won't even be remembered,
because it's all the same, the days, the eves
blur into one bigger blur.
The pen is my anchor
in the waters of wish-wash woe.

I miss you so. I miss you.
We used to stand by oceans deep,
hand in hand, lip on lip, feet upon sandy granules.
I always felt your heartbeat, trip
over itself, giddy with gladness that I was there.

I miss your loving stare,
a stare that now is vacant and blank and bleak.
It speaks to me, saying "I'd rather look somewhere else.
Anywhere else."
But there was a time, our time, when you'd only look
into my blue eyes and nowhere but.
Now I'm blue as that sea we used to listen to through
seashells.

Sometimes I listen and listen and listen,
holding my phone to my ear like those shells.
Instead of an ocean, I think I can hear you.
I'm not expecting your answer anymore;
echoing like waves,
but just the sound of your voice on the machine.
I'll hurriedly hang up, fear frenzying me until I
remember it's November:
a month for lost souls,
empty shells.

My heart, it swells
like ocean currents
but I have to let you go—
I'm like a glass bottle: filled with a message you'll likely
never see as it reaches some foreign shore.
I'm unsure
where you are.
Or when you're making your way up the path
in our suburb of sea.
I just hope one time you pass me,
(maybe some night in November)
and that you remember the time,
our time,
that you and I were 'we'.

lost property

Lately
I've been feeling lost.
Like an item of property
someone's dropped
and forgotten about,
left on a bench:
a wallet or a pair of favourite sunglasses.

The owner hasn't been in contact
with anyone to collect me.
Instead, I sit here,
waiting,
waiting
thinking 'should I get up and move on
or should I stay put so I can be found?'

Maybe I no longer want that:
to be found.
Maybe an ownerless existence
frees up a freedom I never knew.

a portrait of you

She used to favour watercolour,
now she rarely uses blue.
A wish-wash of vibrant colour,
of greens and hazy hues.
It wasn't always clear skies
in the picture perfect frame.
She paints away her Sundays now,
to forget his name.

encore

con amore

"with love"

the words

I remember being so eager to write you down.
Like somehow, I knew, one day I'd be walking with dad,
down God's aisle in the purest gown.
But my hand, how it paused:
the pen not scraping the pages.
Fear, it seems, froze me stiff in those early stages.

Any good writer knows to conquer nerves—
a first page stares and scares;
has you struggling with the words.
But just like the first chapter of a well-written book,
you had me rapidly reading
with your singular, novel look.

It scared me to know that
our story was still unfinished
but as time wrote us onward,
that doubtful dark diminished.
The words, the words they
                f
             l
         o
             wed
                  from my soul
                     to yours.
                 Now all I hear
              are our loved ones,
     showering us with celebratory applause.

                   Let's cut the cake:
                  there's no mistake
                    as now my lips,
               they form the words.

Words that you have heard before
but never quite so pure.

For these vows, these words that drift from my tongue,
proclaim you are my only one:
a risen sun that's lit the dark.
Upon my heart, you've etched
a permanent mark.

We've erased the pencil.
Now written with pen
is a love inked indelibly upon our souls.
Our story so far has all led to when
we now become a united whole.

And our souls
proclaim those vows of ours
for all the days and nights of life.
You forever my husband,
and I: always your wife.

Through all strife
and any sentence,
any page that's hard to turn.
My darling, I will love you
as a light that forever burns.

To love you through the darkness,
a red light always shining.
To be your hope in hopeless moments,
faith in us never resigning.

To care for you with gentle hands,
nurturing with tender touch.
To share with you all I am,
even if I feel it's at times too much.

To be your other with all my strength,
loving with all my soul.
To unite with you and tend to you,
a faithful half of our whole.

To endure through the trials and troubles
that life duly ensures.
To pray for your soul, for a heavenly home,
for God's graces to outpour.

To love not just your best,
but to find compassion for your worst.
To prioritise you before all others,
to place our family first.

To laugh with you through all seasons,
in all weathers and all woes.
To share this life with you no matter what,
no matter how it goes.

I promise

~~little big~~ *girl*

I

Little girl
in that frame,
I wish I could tell you how you've grown.
And how I wish I could speak to you;
tell you about all that is unknown.

Like how, little girl,
you're not always going to be tall.
See, your brother's going to outgrow you.
You'll stand fully-grown at 5 foot 1
on that height-marked wall.
And you won't even be able to wear high heels to fix it
'cos your feet are weirdly, widely shaped.

And little girl
there'll be times
where all you want is to run, is to escape.
You'll walk each morning as soon as you wake
in the same shore-lined suburb you've lived
for all your years.

And your fears
little girl, will still be the dark
but a different depth to it, you didn't know.
Little girl I wish I could warn you of it,
but these things aren't told, rather, they're shown.

Unknown. Unknown. Oh little girl, life's all one big unknown.
But look to love, have faith in God's throne.
You're not ever on your own.

II

Little girl
in that album,
how I wish you could speak to me,
my younger clone.

Tell me all about home,
that dystopian story you wrote during recess
while all your classmates poked fun.
Or maybe the one
where you over-worried, or scraped your knee whilst on the run.

How about the story
of all your deep desires, or all your dreams?
Tell me why you sobbed,
kept score with your family
or why you so angrily screamed.
It seems to me so funny,
so fickle now they seem:
those arguments, those concerns.
The burns
you thought were third degree
but actually barely scolded skin.

III

BIG girl
but little feet.
(Still small enough a size
to be mistaken for school age.)
Are you on the same page
of this story?

I worry
you flick back to the start of the chapter
or the back of the book
to reminisce or to ruminate.
Let's get this straight:
'big' writer,
you feel there's something unsettling or wrong
with the word you're currently on?
You've read this sentence ten times over
or skipped a paragraph to get to the good bit?

IV

Little girl or big girl.
It's only perspective that makes you
young or old,
makes things good or bad,
measures you short or tall.

It's comparison to past and future
that makes you feel

over or

_____

underwhelmed

by it all.
But the reality is:
you're currently 5 foot 1
on that height-marked wall.
Reality is, you're just a girl.

Unfurling as the world may seem,
uncertain as your future may feel.
As happier as the past may appear at times,
remember that the moment you're in now,
that's real.
Enjoy it. Be in it, girl.

V

Woman
looking in that wardrobe mirror.
I see the 'me' of then and of there.
I still have that violin bow in one hand,
a pen in the other,
that same brown, fringe-cut hair.

But I am so proud of you
and aware
of all it took
to finish this self-seeing book.

To soak the words in as they came,
love not only the sunshine, but also the rain.

VI

You've always detested maths,
preferred words (probably still)
but here's the sum
of all that's come
and all that later will.

little girl = big girl = woman

about the author

I.W is a poet, musician and receptionist based in Australia. Her short stories and poems were first published in a local literary journal at the age of 11, and since then, she hasn't stopped writing.

In 2021, she released her debut poetry collection, 'Lifting the Veil'; a work aiming to shed a light on the nature of life and death itself.

This, her second collection of poetry and prose, aims to encompass her love of music and words, imparting that feeling of love we all desire.

fine.

www.ingramcontent.com/pod-product-compliance
Lightning Source LLC
Chambersburg PA
CBHW062053290426
44109CB00027B/2811